Hour of Freedom

Hour of Freedom

American History in Poetry

Compiled by Milton Meltzer

Illustrations by Marc Nadel

Wordsong

Boyds Mills Press

Compilation copyright © 2003 by Milton Meltzer
Illustrations copyright © 2003 by Boyds Mills Press
Cover photo: www.comstock.com

Published by Wordsong
Boyds Mills Press, Inc.
A Highlights Company
815 Church Street
Honesdale, Pennsylvania 18431
Printed in China

Publisher Cataloging-in-Publication Data (U.S.)

Meltzer, Milton.
Hour of freedom : American history in poetry / compiled by Milton Meltzer ;
illustrations by Marc Nadel—1st ed.
[96] p. : ill. ; cm.
Includes index.
Brief biographies of poets included.
Summary: The story of America told through poetry, selected by one of the country's
foremost historians.
ISBN 1-59078-021-3
1. United States — Juvenile poetry. 2. Children's poetry, American. (1. United States — Poetry.
2. American poetry — Collections.) I. Nadel, Marc. II. Title.
811.54 21 PS595.U5M4 2003
2002117180

First edition, 2003
The text of this book is set in 11-point Wilke Roman.

Visit our Web site at www.boydsmillspress.com

10 9 8 7 6 5 4 3 2 1

Epigraph

The Universal Song

Let me go where'er I will,
I hear a sky-born music still:
It sounds from all things old,
It sounds from all things young,
From all that's fair, from all that's foul,
Peals out a cheerful song.
It is not only in the rose,
It is not only in the bird,
Not only where the rainbow glows,
Nor in the song of woman heard,
But in the darkest, meanest things,
There alway, alway something sings.
'Tis not in the high stars alone,
Nor in the cups of budding flowers;
Nor in the redbreast's mellow tone,
Nor in the bow that smiles in showers,
But in the mud and scum of things
There alway, alway something sings.

RALPH WALDO EMERSON

Table of Contents

From Slavery to Freedom

The Expansion of the Nation

Wars

Changing America

Afterword

Biographical Notes on Poets

Acknowledgments

Index of Titles and First Lines

Introduction

HISTORY IS WHAT HAPPENS TO US: to you, to me, to everyone. And it is what we make happen. To the historians we entrust the care of public memory, of ourselves as a nation. What we think of our American heritage is shaped in part by what historians have told us and by our own experience in the way our society functions.

Historians traditionally focused on the people who ruled—kings, presidents, men and women of wealth and power. A new trend opened the study of history from the bottom up. Research continues to reveal the part "ordinary" people play in our history—people of every age, occupation, color, ethnic origin.

But rarely have historians opened their pages to poets. Yet poets' sense of the past, as well as of the life around them, can do much to extend and deepen the range of our own experience. For poets have an intensely personal vision of life. They say to us, "Here is how I have seen and shaped a moment of living, a view of life. Read what I have written, and experience that time of life through my senses and emotions and perceptions."

Poets come alive to a particular event, character, or period of time. Like the rest of us, they don't live only in the present. You'll find that some of the poems in this book convey how the poet felt about an event in the past—not personally observed, yet deeply imagined.

This book includes some writing not commonly thought of as poetry. That is, the lyrics of songs—folk, spirituals, anthems. They are given here without the music composed for them, since the words can stand on their own. Many such lyrics, often by Anonymous, arose out of the shared feeling of a group of people experiencing an historical event or pressure.

Hundreds, no, thousands of poets have written about their lives in what is now known as the United States of America. Their published works are found in many anthologies. This book does not aim at collecting every poem bearing upon historical events. In offering a sampling of poetry's response to history, this volume may encourage you to look for more such songs of experience— and maybe to write some yourself.

The anthology is arranged by time periods—from the colonial era to today's immigration to the United States from almost all parts of the world. The various sections are not precisely timed. Some events or trends carry over for decades or even generations beyond their initial impact. For that reason certain poems could be placed in more than one time period.

Brief notes about the poems or authors, placing the work in context, precede the selections.

I

THE COLONIAL ERA

NORTH AMERICA, SETTLED BY EUROPEANS beginning in 1607, was so vast a territory that in 1750 their communities had yet to cross the Appalachians and penetrate the unknown interior. It took a long time to people the land. In 1650 there were only fifty thousand settlers, huddled mostly in Massachusetts and Virginia. A hundred years later the number had grown to a bit more than one million, stretching from the forests of Maine in the north to the wilds of Georgia in the south.

The immigrants were of many stocks—English, Scottish, Irish, Welsh, Dutch, French, German, Swedish, Swiss, Jewish, and Africans, many brought here in chains to labor in all the colonies, North and South. But early on, the English far outnumbered the other white colonists.

This land was not empty of people when the settlers arrived. Certainly ten thousand years before, and possibly as far back as 35,000 B.C., the aborigines of America, the true first discoverers, had come from northeast Asia and moved southward from what is now Alaska to populate both North and South America. Colonial policy led to the displacement of the Native Americans from various territories.

Most poems of this era are spiritual. Only a few bear directly on the historical events or issues of the day.

Born *nearly two hundred years after the Pilgrims' arrival, the poet mourns the fate of the Native Americans who welcomed the newcomers.*

The Indian's Welcome to the Pilgrim Fathers

Above them spread a stranger sky;
　　Around, the sterile plain;
The rock-bound coast rose frowning nigh;
　　Beyond,—the wrathful main:
Chill remnants of the wintry snow
　　Still choked the encumbered soil,
Yet forth those Pilgrim Fathers go
　　To mark their future toil.

'Mid yonder vale their corn must rise
　　In summer's ripening pride,
And there the church-spire woo the skies
　　Its sister-school beside.
Perchance mid England's velvet green
　　Some tender thought reposed,
Though nought upon their stoic mien
　　Such soft regret disclosed.

When sudden from the forest wide
　　A red-bowed chieftain came,
With towering form, and haughty stride,
　　And eye like kindling flame:
No wrath he breathed, no conflict sought,
　　To no dark ambush drew,
But simply to the Old World brought
　　The welcome of the New.

That welcome was a blast and ban
　　Upon thy race unborn;
Was there no seer,—thou fated Man!—
　　Thy lavish zeal to warn?
Thou in thy fearless faith didst hail
　　A weak, invading band,
But who shall heed thy children's wail
　　Swept from their native land?

Thou gav'st the riches of thy streams,
　　The lordship o'er thy waves,
The region of thine infant dreams
　　And of thy father's graves,—
But who to yon proud mansions, piled
　　With wealth of earth and sea,
Poor outcast from thy forest wild,
　　Say, who shall welcome thee?

Lydia H. Sigourney

The poet finds humor in those infants who, born in colonial times, were unaffected by the hardships and strangeness of the New World.

Peregrine White and Virginia Dare

1620   1587

Peregrine White
And Virginia Dare
Were the first real Americans
Anywhere.

Others might find it
Strange to come
Over the ocean
To make a home,

England and memory
Left behind—
But Virginia and Peregrine
Didn't mind.

One of them born
On Roanoke,
And the other cradled
In Pilgrim oak.

Rogues might bicker
And good men pray.
Did they pay attention?
No, not they.

Men might grumble
And women weep
But Virginia and Peregrine
Went to sleep.

They had their dinner
And napped and then
When they woke up
It was dinner again.

They didn't worry,
They didn't wish,
They didn't farm
And they didn't fish.

There was lots of work
But they didn't do it.
They were pioneers
But they never knew it.

Wolves in the forest
And Indian drums!
Virginia and Peregrine
Sucked their thumbs.

They were only babies.
They didn't care.
Peregrine White
And Virginia Dare.

Stephen Vincent Benét

Native Americans, gradually forced off their lands by the rising tide of immigrants from Europe, had few defenders. Freneau, born in colonial times, imagines their peaceful life beyond the grave, safe from the invaders.

The Indian Burying Ground

In spite of all the learned have said,
    I still my old opinion keep;
The *posture*, that *we* give the dead,
    Points out the soul's eternal sleep.

Not so the ancients of these lands—
    The Indian, when from life released,
Again is seated with his friends,
    And shares again the joyous feast.

His imaged birds, and painted bowl,
    And venison, for a journey dressed,
Bespeak the nature of the soul,
    ACTIVITY, that knows no rest.

His bow, for action ready bent,
    And arrows, with a head of stone,
Can only mean that life is spent,
    And not the old ideas gone.

Thou, stranger, that shalt come this way,
    No fraud upon the dead commit—
Observe the swelling turf, and say
    They do not *lie,* but here they *sit.*

Here still a lofty rock remains,
    On which the curious eye may trace
(Now wasted, half, by wearing rains)
    The fancies of a ruder race.

Here still an aged elm aspires,
    Beneath whose far-projecting shade
(And which the Shepherd still admires)
    The children of the forest played!

There oft a restless Indian queen
    (Pale *Shebah,* with her braided hair)
And many a barbarous form is seen
    To chide the man that lingers there.

By midnight moons, o'er moistening dews,
    In habit for the chase arrayed,
The hunter still the deer pursues,
    The hunter and the deer, a shade!

And long shall timorous fancy see
    The painted chief, and pointed spear,
And Reason's self shall bow the knee
    To shadows and delusions here.

PHILIP FRENEAU

B*reaking with traditional forms of verse, Sandburg conveys immense meaning in just two sentences.*

Circles

The white man drew a small circle in the sand
and told the red man, "This is what the Indian
knows," and drawing a big circle around the
small one, "This is what the white man knows."
The Indian took the stick and swept an immense
ring around both circles: "This is where the
white man and the red man know nothing."

CARL SANDBURG

II

THE STRUGGLE FOR INDEPENDENCE

‹⁂›

AS THE COLONIES GREW LARGER in population and gained more economic strength, troubles developed between them and the home country. Great Britain acted like a parent ruling its child, while the Americans contended they were big enough to decide their own course. Britain gave orders to control the economic life of the colonies in ways that would profit the home country at the expense of the Americans. But money was not the only source of conflict. Government—who gave orders and who had to obey them—was another source. Many colonists believed they were being taxed without having any say in how much and for what purposes.

In 1755 conflict between Britain and France over world domination erupted in a long war on the North American continent. The Americans fought alongside the British to win a victory that added vast territory to the empire. The colonies learned to cooperate with one another in the hard struggle. The colonists believed that they no longer needed to depend on Britain to defend themselves.

New sources of trouble quickly appeared. Who would govern the western lands just acquired by conquest? Who would pay the war debt? Why couldn't the colonies trade with anyone they liked, instead of trading only with England?

And above all, why couldn't the colonies make their own decisions? Why should the British Parliament make all the decisions on colonial matters when the colonies were denied any voice in that Parliament?

More and more, angry voices were raised in the colonial assemblies. In the 1760s Parliament passed taxation measures that added fuel to the fires of protest. Patrick Henry in Virginia introduced resolutions asserting no one but the assembly had the right to lay taxes upon the colony. "If this be treason, make the most of it!" he cried out.

Other colonies soon followed his lead. Britain backed off a bit as the protests mounted, but the colonies kept moving down the road from resistance to revolution. The Boston Massacre (1770) and the Boston Tea Party (1773) were acts of defiance that infuriated the British government. In 1774 delegates from the colonies met in Philadelphia in the first Continental Congress. They demanded the repeal of all of Parliament's offensive acts and the right to shape their own future.

The delegates knew these acts made war possible. If it were to come, however, the British would have to start it. On April 19, 1775, a British general in Boston sent one thousand troops to capture a store of munitions in Concord, Massachusetts, hidden by farmers and villagers organized as "Minutemen." Learning of the troops' destination, Paul Revere and William Dawes rode out to carry the alarm to the countryside.

The militiamen swarmed to the defense. In the fighting that erupted at Concord and Lexington, Massachusetts, seventy-three British soldiers were killed and many more were wounded; the American losses were ninety-three dead, wounded, or missing.

The American Revolution had begun. The Second Continental Congress met in Philadelphia and chose George Washington to be chief of the Continental forces. In July 1776 the delegates in the congress voted for the Declaration of Independence drawn up by Thomas Jefferson of Virginia.

Against great odds—an infant nation matching itself against the world's richest power with the strongest army and navy—Washington's troops fought a long, drawn-out war that climaxed in October 1781, when Lord Cornwallis surrendered his entire army of seven thousand men at Yorktown. A peace treaty signed on September 3, 1783, signified Britain's acceptance of the colonies as an independent nation, the United States of America.

*C*oncord, Massachusetts, was a major supply depot for the colonial militia. When the British tried to seize it on April 19, 1775, a battle took place at the town's North Bridge, now a national park. Emerson, a Concord resident, wrote this poem for the dedication of the Battle Monument.

Concord Hymn

Sung at the completion of the Battle Monument, July 4, 1837

By the rude bridge that arched the flood,
    Their flag to April's breeze unfurled,
Here once the embattled farmers stood,
    And fired the shot heard round the world.

The foe long since in silence slept;
    Alike the conqueror silent sleeps;
And Time the ruined bridge has swept
    Down the dark stream which seaward creeps.

On this green bank, by this soft stream,
    We set today a votive stone;
That memory may their deed redeem,
    When, like our sires, our sons are gone.

Spirit, that made those heroes dare
    To die, and leave their children free,
Bid Time and Nature gently spare
    The shaft we raise to them and thee.

RALPH WALDO EMERSON

A *legendary figure of the American Revolution, Molly Pitcher was not the only woman to fight the British alongside men. Some, wearing men's clothing, got through the war without being detected as female.*

Molly Pitcher

All day the great guns barked and roared;
All day the big balls screeched and soared;
All day, 'mid the sweating gunners grim,
Who toiled in their smoke-shroud dense and dim,
Sweet Molly labored with courage high,
With steady hand and watchful eye,
Till the day was ours, and the sinking sun
Looked down on the field of Monmouth won,
And Molly standing beside her gun.

Now, Molly, rest your weary arm!
Safe, Molly, all is safe from harm.
Now, woman, bow your aching head,
And weep in sorrow o'er your dead!

Next day on that field so hardly won,
Stately and calm stands Washington,
And looks where our gallant Greene doth lead
A figure clad in motley weed—
A soldier's cap and a soldier's coat
Masking a woman's petticoat.
He greets our Molly in kindly wise;
He bids her raise her tearful eyes;
And now he hails her before them all
Comrade and soldier, whate'er befall,
"And since she has played a man's full part,
A man's reward for her loyal heart!
And Sergeant Molly Pitcher's name
Be writ henceforth on the shield of fame!"

Oh, Molly, with your eyes so blue!
Oh, Molly, Molly, here's to you!
Sweet honor's roll will aye be richer
To hold the name of Molly Pitcher.

LAURA E. RICHARDS

Sentiment for a break with Great Britain had mounted. Meeting in Philadelphia, the Continental Congress asked Thomas Jefferson, working with a committee, to draft a Declaration of Independence. An anonymous poet wrote these stanzas to capture the wild excitement of the crowd outside the hall, awaiting the vote for liberty.

Liberty Bell

There was tumult in the city,
In the quaint old Quaker town,
And the streets were rife with people,
Pacing restless up and down,
People gathering at corners,
Where they whispered, each to each,
And the sweat stood on their temples,
With the earnestness of speech.

As the bleak Atlantic currents
Lash the wild Newfoundland shore,
So they beat against the State House,
So they surged against the door;

And the mingling of their voices
Made a harmony profound,
Till the quiet street of Chestnut
Was all turbulent with sound.

"Will they do it?"—"Dare they do it?"
"Who is speaking?"—"What's the news?" —
"What of Adams?"—"What of Sherman?" —
"Oh, God grant they won't refuse!"—

Aloft in that high steeple
Sat the bellman, old and gray;
He was weary of the tyrant
And his iron-sceptered sway;
So he sat with one hand ready
On the clapper of the bell,
When his eye should catch the signal,
Very happy news to tell.

See! see! the dense crowd quivers
Through all its lengthy line,
As the boy beside the portal
Looks forth to give the sign.
With his small hands upward lifted,
Breezes dallying with his hair,
Hark! with deep, clear intonation,
Breaks his young voice on the air.

Hushed the people's swelling murmur,
List the boy's strong, joyous cry—
"*Ring!*" he shouts aloud, "*Ring, Grandpa!*
Ring! Oh, ring for Liberty!"
And, straightway, at the signal,
The old bellman lifts his hand,
And sends the good news, making
Iron music through the land.

How they shouted! What rejoicing!
How the old bell shook the air,
Till the clang of Freedom ruffled
The calm, gliding Delaware!
How the bonfires and the torches
Illumed the night's repose!
And from the flames, like Phoenix,
Fair Liberty arose!

That old bell now is silent,
And hushed its iron tongue,
But the spirit it awakened
Still lives—forever young.
And, while we greet the sunlight,
On the fourth of each July,
We'll ne'er forget the bellman
Who, 'twixt the earth and sky,
Rung out OUR INDEPENDENCE;
Which, please God, *shall never die!*

ANONYMOUS

*O*n October 19, 1781, the British army, under Lord Cornwallis, surrendered to the American forces at Yorktown in Virginia. With that defeat, British hopes for crushing the American Revolution collapsed.

Lord Cornwallis' Surrender

Come all ye brave Americans,
    The Truth to you I'll tell,
'Tis of a sad misfortune,
    To Britain late befell,
'Twas all in the heights of Yorktown,
    Where cannon loud did roar —
They summoned Lord Cornwallis
    To fight or else give o'er.

The summons then to be served
    Was sent unto my Lord,
Which made him feel like poor Burgoyne,
    And quickly draw his sword.
Say, must I give these glittering troops,
    These ships and Hessians too,
And yield to Gen'ral Washington
    And his bold rebel crew?

A grand council then was called,
    His Lordship gave command,
Say, what think you now, my heroes,
    To yield you may depend—
For don't you see the bomb shells fly,
    And cannons loud do roar,
Count de Grasse lies in the harbor,
    And Washington's on shore.

'Twas the nineteenth of October,
    In the year eighty-one,
Lord Cornwallis he surrender'd
    To General Washington:
They marched from their posts, brave boys,
    And quickly grounded arms,

Rejoice, ye brave Americans,
    With music's sweetest charms.

Six thousand chosen British troops
    To Washington resign'd,
Besides some ships and Hessians,
    That could not stay behind;
With refugees and blackamores;
    O what a direful crew!
It was then he had some thousands,
    But now he's got but few.

My Lord has gone unto New York,
    Sir Harry for to see;
For to send home this dreadful news
    Unto His Majesty;
To contradict some former lines,
    That once to him was sent,
That he and his bold British troops,
    They conquered where they went.

Here's a healthy to great Washington,
    And his brave army too,
And likewise to our worthy Greene,
    To him much honor's due.
May we subdue those English troops,
    And clear the eastern shore,
That we may live in peace, my boys,
    Whilst wars they are no more.

                    ANONYMOUS

By the time the poet Lowell grew into manhood, it was clear to him that independence from Great Britain did not stop the need to struggle for an end to poverty and slavery.

Our Fathers Fought for Liberty

Our fathers fought for liberty,
They struggled long and well,
History of their deeds can tell—
But did they leave us free?

Are we free to speak our thought,
To be happy and be poor,
Free to enter Heaven's door,
To live and labor as we ought?

Are we then made free at last
From the fear of what men say.
Free to reverence today,
Free from the slavery of the past?

Our fathers fought for liberty,
They struggled long and well,
History of their deeds can tell—
But *ourselves* must set us free.

JAMES RUSSELL LOWELL

U.S. cities and towns—and a state—were named after the Father of Our Country, and many portraits and statues of him have been created over time. But the Washington Monument in the nation's capital is probably the dominant symbol of George Washington's greatness.

Washington Monument by Night

The stone goes straight.
A lean swimmer dives into night sky,
Into half-moon mist.

Two trees are coal black.
This is a great white ghost between.
It is cool to look at.
Strong men, strong women, come here.

Eight years is a long time
To be fighting all the time.

The republic is a dream.
Nothing happens unless first a dream.

The wind bit hard at Valley Forge one
   Christmas.
Soldiers tied rags on their feet.
Red footprints wrote on the snow . . .
. . . and stone shoots into stars here
. . . into half-moon mist tonight.

Tongues wrangled dark at a man.
He buttoned his overcoat and stood alone.
In a snowstorm, red hollyberries, thoughts,
   he stood alone.

Women said: He is lonely
. . . fighting . . . fighting . . . eight years . . .

The name of an iron man goes over the world.
It takes a long time to forget an iron man.

CARL SANDBURG

*T*homas Jefferson, author of the Declaration of Independence and third
president of the United States, is celebrated in song for his ringing call for liberty.

Jefferson and Liberty

The gloomy night before us flies,
The reign of terror now is o'er;
Its gags, inquisitors and spies,
Its herds of Harpies are no more.

(CHORUS)
Rejoice, Columbia's sons, rejoice;
To tyrants never bend the knee;
But join with heart and soul and voice,
For Jefferson and liberty.

No lordling here with gorging jaws
Shall wring from industry the food,
Nor fiery bigot's holy laws
Lay waste our fields and streets in blood!
(Chorus)

Here strangers from a thousand shores
Compelled by tyranny to roam,
Shall find, amidst abundant stores
A nobler and a happier home.
(Chorus)

Here Art shall lift her laurel'd head,
Wealth, Industry, and Peace divine;
And where dark, pathless forests spread,
Rich fields and lofty cities shine.
(Chorus)

ANONYMOUS

The Constitution's performance in the War of 1812 earned the forty-four-gun frigate the nickname of Old Ironsides. The poem, written when Holmes was twenty years old, swept the country. Along with penny donations from millions of American children, the poem helped save the old battleship from threatened destruction. Today it is anchored in Boston Harbor.

Old Ironsides

Ay, tear her tattered ensign down!
    Long has it waved on high,
And many an eye has danced to see
    That banner in the sky;
Beneath it rung the battle shout,
    And burst the cannon's roar;—
The meteor of the ocean air
    Shall sweep the clouds no more.

Her deck, once red with heroes' blood,
    Where knelt the vanquished foe,
When winds were hurrying o'er the flood,
    And waves were white below,
No more shall feel the victor's tread,
    Or know the conquered knee;—
The harpies of the shore shall pluck
    The eagle of the sea!

Oh better that her shattered hulk
    Should sink beneath the wave;
Her thunders shook the mighty deep,
    And there should be her grave;
Nail to the mast her holy flag,
    Set every threadbare sail,
And give her to the god of storms,
    The lightning and the gale!

OLIVER WENDELL HOLMES

From our earliest years, in school or out, we hear these lyrics sung, and many hold them in memory forever after.

America

My country, 'tis of thee,
Sweet land of liberty,
Of thee I sing;
Land where my fathers died,
Land of the Pilgrim's pride,
From ev'ry mountainside
Let freedom ring!

My native country, thee,
Land of the noble free,
Thy name I love;
I love thy rocks and rills,
Thy woods and templed hills;
My heart with rapture thrills,
Like that above.

Let music swell the breeze,
And ring from all the trees
Sweet freedom's song.
Let mortal tongues awake;
Let all that breathe partake;
Let rocks their silence break,
The sound prolong.

Our father's God, to Thee,
Author of liberty,
To Thee we sing.
Long may our land be bright
With freedom's holy light;
Protect us by Thy might,
Great God, our King!

SAMUEL FRANCIS SMITH

III

YOUNG AMERICA

THE PROMISE OF THE YOUNG REPUBLIC inspired the new Americans. People hoped and prayed for the fulfillment of those "self-evident truths" written into the Declaration of Independence: "that all men are created equal, that they are endowed by their Creator with certain unalienable rights, that among these are life, liberty, and the pursuit of happiness."

The first step was to decide how the new nation would be governed. Delegates from all the states met in 1787 to draw up a Constitution that would replace the weak Articles of Confederation drafted during the Revolutionary War. Out of their deliberations came a document whose wisdom, practical ingenuity, and vitality armed the new nation for a turbulent future. A Bill of Rights was added in 1791, guaranteeing freedoms for individuals that no government could take away.

The population kept expanding by natural increase and by continued immigration. Still, by 1840 the part of the continent that comprised the nation was only thinly settled. The total number was seventeen million: Approximately ten million lived on the Atlantic slope, six million in the Mississippi Valley, and one million along the Gulf of Mexico. The nation was organized into twenty-six states and three territories (Florida, Iowa, and Wisconsin). The "West" in those early days was much closer.

The great majority of the people lived on farms. In the North most farms were owned by the families that worked them. In the South large plantations predominated with black slaves, who labored in work gangs to raise commercial crops of cotton, sugar, rice, indigo, or tobacco.

New York was the nation's biggest city with three hundred thousand inhabitants. Next in size came Philadelphia, Boston, and New Orleans. American authors Longfellow, Lowell, Whittier, Holmes, Poe, Bryant, Cooper, Melville, and Hawthorne had begun to write poetry and fiction that would long endure. But most readers turned first to the penny newspapers, providing fresh news every day.

This was a time when a tide of reform was flooding the country. Men and women, singly or as part of newly formed organizations, took up the battle against privilege and injustice. They fought against factories that employed women and children.

People traveled by stagecoach, by ship, by foot, or by horse. They pushed farther into the heart of the vast continent. A few new railroads tooted between points, and new waterways, such as the Erie Canal, spurred commerce and emigration west. West—people wanted above all to go west. They had many motives, but the strongest was hunger for land. Southern planters and politicians looked for ways to expand their slave territory and thus, too, their influence in Congress.

Nature's gifts to the vast American continent may have been abundant, but the poet believed that, early on, it was the nation's teachers who steered the country in the right direction.

America Was Schoolmasters

America was forests,
America was grain,
Wheat from dawn to sunset,
And rainbows trailing rain.

America was beavers,
Buffalo in seas,
Cornsilk and the johnnycake,
Songs of scythes and bees.

America was brown men
With eyes full of the sun,
But America was schoolmasters,
Tall one by lonely one.

They hewed oak, carried water,
Their hands were knuckleboned,
They piled on loads of syntax
Till the small boys groaned.

They taught the girls such manners
As stiffened them for life,
But made many a fine speller,
Good mother and good wife.

They took small wiry children,
Wild as panther-cats,
And turned them into reasoning,
Sunny democrats.

They caught a nation eager,
They caught a nation young,
They taught the nation fairness,
Thrift, and the golden tongue.

They started at the bottom
And built up strong and sweet,
They shaped our minds and morals
With switches on the seat!

ROBERT P. TRISTRAM COFFIN

Sandburg was born as the vast herds of buffalo in the West were disappearing, slaughtered by hunters for profit and by trainmen anxious to clear the newly laid railroad tracks. All were heedless to the dependence of Native Americans on these enormous beasts for food and clothing.

Buffalo Dusk

The buffaloes are gone.
And those who saw the buffaloes are gone.
Those who saw the buffaloes by thousands and
    how they pawed the prairie sod into dust
    with their hoofs, their great heads down
    pawing on in a great pageant of dusk,
Those who saw the buffaloes are gone.
And the buffaloes are gone.

CARL SANDBURG

The vast westward migration of Americans eager for a better and more prosperous life was so dramatic an epic that it has inspired the writing of poems, novels, plays, movies, and television shows from decades past through today.

Western Wagons

They went with axe and rifle, when the trail was still to blaze,
They went with wife and children, in the prairie-schooner days,
With banjo and with frying pan—Susanna, don't you cry!
For I'm off to California to get rich out there or die!

We've broken land and cleared it, but we're tired of where we are.
They say that wild Nebraska is a better place by far.
There's gold in far Wyoming, there's black earth in Ioway,
So pack up the kids and blankets, for we're moving out today!

The cowards never started and the weak died on the road,
And all across the continent the endless campfires glowed.
We'd taken land and settled—but a traveler passed by—
And we're going West tomorrow—Lordy, never ask us why!

We're going West tomorrow, where the promises can't fail.
O'er the hills in legions, boys, and crowd the dusty trail!
We shall strive and freeze and suffer. We shall die, and tame the lands.
But we're going West tomorrow, with our fortune in our hands.

STEPHEN VINCENT BENÉT

Bryant's devotion to his native land and his affection for the physical world stir the imagination of readers who may have never seen the prairies.

from The Prairies

These are the gardens of the Desert, these
The unshorn fields, boundless and beautiful,
For which the speech of England has no name—
The Prairies. I behold them for the first,
And my heart swells, while the dilated sight
Takes in the encircling vastness. Lo! they stretch,
In airy undulations, far away,
As if the ocean, in his gentlest swell,
Stood still, with all his rounded billows fixed,
And motionless forever.—Motionless?—
No—they are all unchained again. The clouds
Sweep over with their shadows, and, beneath,
The surface rolls and fluctuates to the eye;
Dark hollows seem to glide along and chase
The sunny ridges. . . .

Still this great solitude is quick with life.
Myriads of insects, gaudy as the flowers
They flutter over, gentle quadrupeds,
And birds, that scarce have learned the fear of man,
Are here, and sliding reptiles of the ground,
Startlingly beautiful. The graceful deer
Bounds to the wood at my approach. The bee,
A more adventurous colonist than man,
With whom he came across the eastern deep,
Fills the savannas with his murmurings,
And hides his sweets, as in the golden age,
Within the hollow oak. I listen long
To his domestic hum, and think I hear
The sound of that advancing multitude
Which soon shall fill these deserts. From the ground
Comes up the laugh of children, the soft voice
Of maidens, and the sweet and solemn hymn
Of Sabbath worshippers. The low of herds
Blends with the rustling of the heavy grain
Over the dark brown furrow. All at once
A fresher wind sweeps by, and breaks my dream,
And I am in the wilderness alone.

WILLIAM CULLEN BRYANT

The railroad—and progress—meant nothing to Thoreau, who favored the natural world.

What's the Railroad

What's the railroad to me?
I never go to see
Where it ends.
It fills a few hollows,
And makes banks for the swallows,
It sets the sand a-blowing,
And the blackberries a-growing.

HENRY DAVID THOREAU

The Erie Canal, which opened in 1825, stretched across New York State from Albany to Buffalo and linked the Hudson River with Lake Erie. It prompted the flow of commerce eastward and the movement of European immigrants to the west.

The Erie Canal

Yet, it is not that Wealth now enriches the scene,
Where the treasures of Art, and of Nature, convene;
'Tis not that this union (of waters) our coffers may fill—
O! no—it is something more exquisite still.

'Tis, that Genius has triumph'd—and Science prevail'd,
Tho' Prejudice flouted, and Envy assail'd,
It is, that the vassals of Europe may see
The progress of mind, in a land that is free.

SAMUEL WOODWORTH

*T*hese lines from Whitman's poetry book Leaves of Grass *reveal the glory he found in everyday things. At the age of thirty-six, in 1855, he self-published the first edition.*

I Hear America Singing

I hear America singing, the varied carols I hear,
Those of mechanics, each one singing his as it should be blithe and strong,
The carpenter singing his as he measures his plank or beam,
The mason singing his as he makes ready for work, or leaves off work,
The boatman singing what belongs to him in his boat, the deckhand singing on
    the steamboat deck,
The shoemaker singing as he sits on his bench, the hatter singing as he stands,
The wood-cutter's song, the ploughboy's on his way in the morning, or at noon
    intermission or at sundown,
The delicious singing of the mother, or of the young wife at work, or of the girl
    sewing or washing,
Each singing what belongs to him or her and to none else,
The day what belongs to the day—at night the party of young fellows,
    robust, friendly,
Singing with open mouths their strong melodious songs.

WALT WHITMAN

IV

FROM SLAVERY TO FREEDOM

—◆—◇◆◇—◆—

THE UNITED STATES VICTORY OVER MEXICO in the war of 1846–1847 was a turning point in history. The enormous territorial growth (adding what would become California, New Mexico, Arizona, Nevada, Colorado, and Utah) led the North and South to quarrel bitterly over the future of the new lands. Would the states carved out of the new territories become slave or free? Antislavery congressmen campaigned to keep the new territories free. Southerners feared that if the antislavery congressmen succeeded, the spread of slavery would be checked and the political power of the slave states doomed.

In the election campaigns of the 1840s and 1850s, a showdown between the antislavery and proslavery forces came nearer. The threat of disunion, voiced often in the fevered debate, alarmed many citizens. The Compromise of 1850, intended to end the issue, contained a Fugitive Slave Law compelling the return of runaway slaves to their masters.

The Supreme Court's Dred Scott Decision of 1857 declared that blacks were "so far inferior that they had no rights which the white man was bound to respect," denying all hope of justice for African Americans. White voters in ever greater numbers were driven toward the antislavery movement.

In the election of 1860 Abraham Lincoln won the presidency. He stood on a platform against any further extension of the slave system. Six weeks later, the slave states, one after another, began to secede from the

Union. They established the Confederate States of America and elected Jefferson Davis of Mississippi as its president. When Confederate forces fired on Fort Sumter in April 1861, the Civil War began.

That war, lasting four long years, would cost more lives than all American wars to date. At first, blacks were denied the right to fight for their own freedom. After Lincoln's Emancipation Proclamation of January 1, 1863, Union ranks were opened to African Americans, and they joined up eagerly. Although promises of equal treatment were not kept, they fought hard and well. By the war's end, 180,000 blacks had served in Lincoln's army and 30,000 in the navy, while 250,000 helped the military as laborers. To put an end to slavery, 38,000 blacks gave their lives in battle. Twenty-one received the Congressional Medal of Honor. The war ended in a Northern victory in April 1865. Five days later, President Lincoln, who had been elected to a second term of office, was assassinated by John Wilkes Booth while attending the theater. Walt Whitman mourned his death in "O Captain, My Captain."

Congress then passed constitutional amendments that changed the status of African Americans. The Thirteenth Amendment abolished slavery, the Fourteenth asserted the equal citizenship of all blacks, and the Fifteenth guaranteed suffrage for all male citizens, regardless of race or color.

The needs of the freed people were great. They wanted work and wages, food and clothing, a roof overhead, education for themselves and their children. They could not look to former slaveholders for help, for some whites were bitterly hostile in the disaster of defeat.

For a brief time, blacks and whites in the South lived under conditions established by acts of Congress to reconstruct the war-torn region.

But after scarcely a dozen years, Reconstruction ended. Many problems were left unsolved, especially how to provide land for the freed black farmers. Northern business interests now dominated the government. When federal troops, which had been protecting blacks, were withdrawn from the South, blacks once more stood deserted and alone. Their rights were torn away. But blacks and freedom-loving whites still hoped for equality for all.

G*arrison, editor of the abolitionist journal* The Liberator, *wrote this poem in 1832, anticipating the joyous time when freedom would be won—which was realized more than three decades later.*

The Hour of Freedom

The hour of freedom! come it must.
    O hasten it, in mercy, Heaven!
When all who grovel in the dust
    Shall stand erect, their fetters riven;

When glorious freedom shall be won
    By every caste, complexion, clime;
When tyranny shall be o'erthrown,
    And *color* cease to be a *crime*.

WILLIAM LLOYD GARRISON

This is one of many song lyrics created by unknown African Americans to express their condition in slavery.

———— ≈◊≈ ————

Many Thousand Gone

No more auction block for me,
No more, no more;
No more auction block for me,
Many thousand gone.

No more peck o' corn for me,
No more, no more;
No more peck o' corn for me,
Many thousand gone.

No more driver's lash for me,
No more, no more;
No more driver's lash for me,
Many thousand gone.

No more pint o' salt for me,
No more, no more;
No more pint o' salt for me,
Many thousand gone.

No more hundred lash for me,
No more, no more;
No more hundred lash for me,
Many thousand gone.

No more mistress' call for me,
No more, no more;
No more mistress' call for me,
Many thousand gone.

ANONYMOUS

Whitman, *like many others of his time, despised the Fugitive Slave Law of 1850, meant to force citizens to return runaway slaves to their masters. This poem, from* Leaves of Grass, *voices Whitman's spirit of defiance.*

The Runaway Slave

The runaway slave came to my house and stopped outside,
I heard his motions crackling the twigs of the woodpile,
Through the swung half-door of the kitchen I saw him limpsy and weak,
And went where he sat on a log and led him in and assured him,
And brought water and filled a tub for his sweated body and bruised feet,
And gave him a room that entered from my own, and gave him some coarse clean clothes,
And remember perfectly well his revolving eyes and his awkwardness,
And remember putting plasters on the galls of his neck and ankles;
He stayed with me a week before he was recuperated and passed north,
I had him sit next me at table, my firelock leaned in the corner.

WALT WHITMAN

Born a free black, Solomon Northup of Saratoga Springs, New York, was kidnapped from the North and enslaved for twelve years in Louisiana. After his freedom was restored in 1853, he wrote a superb account of his life called Twelve Years a Slave. *Dove conveys his story in this contemporary poem. (His last name is often spelled "Northrup.")*

The Abduction

The bells, the cannons, the houses black with crepe,
all for the great Harrison! The citizenry of Washington
clotted the avenue—I among them, Solomon Northrup
from Saratoga Springs, free papers in my pocket, violin
under arm, my new friends Brown and Hamilton by my side.

Why should I have doubted them? The wages were good.
While Brown's tall hat collected pennies at the tent flap,
Hamilton's feet did a jig on a tightrope,
pigs squealed invisibly from the bleachers and I fiddled.

I remember how the windows rattled with each report.
Then the wine, like a pink lake, tipped.
I was lifted—the sky swivelled, clicked into place.

I floated on water I could not drink. Though the pillow
was stone, I climbed no ladders in that sleep.

I woke and found myself alone, in darkness and in chains.

RITA DOVE

One of Whittier's popular ballads, this commemorates the brave ninety-year-old woman (perhaps a composite of several women) who defied Confederate troops when they tried to force her to lower the American flag.

+——⚹——+

Barbara Frietchie

Up from the meadows rich with corn,
Clear in the cool September morn,

The clustered spires of Frederick stand
Green-walled by the hills of Maryland.

Round about them orchards sweep,
Apple and peach tree fruited deep,

Fair as the garden of the Lord
To the eyes of the famished rebel horde,

On that pleasant morn of the early fall
When Lee marched over the mountain wall;

Over the mountains winding down,
Horse and foot, into Frederick town.

Forty flags with their silver stars,
Forty flags with their crimson bars,

Flapped in the morning wind: the sun
Of noon looked down, and saw not one.

Up rose old Barbara Frietchie then,
Bowed with her fourscore years and ten;

Bravest of all in Frederick town,
She took up the flag the men hauled down;

In her attic window the staff she set,
To show that one heart was loyal yet.

Up the street came the rebel tread,
Stonewall Jackson riding ahead.

Under his slouched hat left and right
He glanced; the old flag met his sight.

"Halt!"—the dust-brown ranks stood fast,
"Fire!"—out blazed the rifle-blast.

It shivered the window, pane and sash;
It rent the banner with seam and gash.

Quick as it fell, from the broken staff
Dame Barbara snatched the silken scarf.

She leaned far out on the window-sill,
And shook it forth with a royal will.

"Shoot, if you must, this old gray head,
But spare your country's flag," she said.

A shade of sadness, a blush of shame,
Over the face of the leader came;

The nobler nature within him stirred
To life at that woman's deed and word;

"Who touches a hair of yon gray head
Dies like a dog! March on!" he said.

All day long through Frederick street
Sounded the tread of marching feet:

All day long that free flag tossed
Over the heads of the rebel host.

Ever its torn folds rose and fell
On the loyal winds that loved it well;

And through the hill-gaps sunset light
Shone over it with a warm good-night.

Barbara Frietchie's work is o'er,
And the Rebel rides on his raids no more.

Honor to her! and let a tear
Fall, for her sake, on Stonewall's bier.

Over Barbara Frietchie's grave,
Flag of Freedom and Union, wave!

Peace and order and beauty draw
Round thy symbol of light and law;

And ever the stars above look down
On thy stars below in Frederick town!

John Greenleaf Whittier

*E*arly in July 1863, the Union forces defeated the Confederates in a major battle at Gettysburg, Pennsylvania. More than seven thousand soldiers were killed. On November 19, fifteen thousand people gathered to dedicate the military cemetery at the battlefield, now a national park. President Lincoln, who had been asked to say just a few words, gave this address—270 words—which took scarcely two minutes. It is a masterpiece of musical language and is treated here as a poem. It expresses the profound conviction of Lincoln, and all the people for whom he spoke, that the American experiment in democracy must not be allowed to fail.

The Gettysburg Address

Fourscore and seven years ago,
our fathers brought forth
on this continent
a new nation,
conceived in Liberty
and dedicated to the proposition
that all men
are created equal.

Now we are engaged
in a great civil war,
testing whether that nation,
or any nation so conceived
and so dedicated,
can long endure.

We are met on a great battlefield
of that war.
We have come to dedicate a portion
of that field, as a final resting place
for those who here gave their lives that
that nation might live.
It is altogether fitting and proper
that we should do this.

But, in a larger sense,
we can not dedicate—
we can not consecrate—
we can not hallow—
this ground.

The brave men,
living and dead, who struggled here
have consecrated it far above
our poor power to add or detract.

The world will little note nor long remember
what we say here, but it can never forget
what they did here.

It is for us the living, rather,
to be dedicated here
to the unfinished work which they
who fought here have thus far so nobly advanced.

It is rather for us to be here
dedicated to the great task remaining before us—
that from these honored dead we take increased devotion
to that cause for which they gave
the last full measure of devotion—
that we here highly resolve
that these dead shall not
have died in vain—
that this nation,
under God,
shall have a new birth of freedom—
and that government
of the people,
by the people,
for the people,
shall not perish
from the earth.

ABRAHAM LINCOLN

This African American poet captures the excitement of the freed people who, for the first time, were given a chance at schooling when Northern teachers came to the South to help during Reconstruction.

Learning to Read

Very soon the Yankee teachers
 Came down and set up school;
But, oh! how the Rebs did hate it,—
 It was agin' their rule.

Our masters always tried to hide
 Book learning from our eyes;
Knowledge didn't agree with slavery—
 T'would make us all too wise.

But some of us would try to steal
 A little from the book,
And put the words together,
 And learn by hook or crook.

I remember Uncle Caldwell,
 Who took pot-liquor fat
And greased the pages of his book,
 And hid it in his hat.

And had his master ever seen
 The leaves upon his head,
He'd have thought them greasy papers,
 But nothing to be read.

And there was Mr. Turner's Ben,
 Who heard the children spell,
And picked the words right up by heart,
 And learned to read 'em well.

Well, the Northern folks kept sending
 The Yankee teachers down;
And they stood right up and helped us,
 Though Rebs did sneer and frown.

And, I longed to read my Bible,
 For precious words it said;
But when I begun to learn it,
 Folks just shook their heads,

And said there is no use trying,
 Oh! Chloe, you're too late;
But as I was rising sixty,
 I had no time to wait.

So I got a pair of glasses,
 And straight to work I went,
And never stopped till I could read
 The hymns and Testament.

Then I got a little cabin—
 A place to call my own—
And I felt as independent
 As the queen upon her throne.

FRANCES ELLEN WATKINS HARPER

D*unbar, whose mother had been a slave, grew up at a time when Reconstruction in the South had ended, and racism, segregation, and discrimination pervaded the North as well.*

Sympathy

I know what the caged bird feels, alas!
    When the sun is bright on the upland slopes;
When the wind stirs soft through the springing grass,
And the river flows like a stream of glass;
    When the first bird sings and the first bud opes,
And the faint perfume from its chalice steals—
I know what the caged bird feels!

I know why the caged bird beats his wing
    Till its blood is red on the cruel bars;
For he must fly back to his perch and cling
When he fain would be on the bough a-swing;
    And a pain still throbs in the old, old scars
And they pulse again with a keener sting—
I know why he beats his wing!

I know why the caged bird sings, ah me,
    When his wing is bruised and his bosom sore,—
When he beats his bars and would be free;
It is not a carol of joy or glee,
    But a prayer that he sends from his heart's deep core,
But a plea, that upward to Heaven, he flings—
I know why the caged bird sings!

PAUL LAURENCE DUNBAR

Whitman was in New York City when he heard that President Lincoln had been assassinated at Ford's Theater in Washington, D.C., on April 14, 1865. He would write two poems to express his grief. The best-known is this one. (The other, one of his greatest, is "When Lilacs Last in the Dooryard Bloom'd.") The singsong rhyme of "O Captain! My Captain!" has been memorized and recited by students for generations. Near the end of his life, the poet said he was sorry he ever wrote it, for whenever he spoke, audiences almost always insisted that he recite it.

O Captain! My Captain!

O Captain! my Captain! our fearful trip is done;
The ship has weathered every rack, the prize we sought is won;
The port is near, the bells I hear, the people all exulting,
While follow eyes the steady keel, the vessel grim and daring:
    But O heart! heart! heart!
        O the bleeding drops of red,
            Where on the deck my Captain lies,
                Fallen cold and dead.
O Captain! my Captain! rise up and hear the bells;
Rise up—for you the flag is flung—for you the bugle trills;
For you bouquets and ribbon'd wreaths—for you the shores a-crowding;
For you they call, the swaying mass, their eager faces turning:
    Here Captain! dear father!
        This arm beneath your head!
            It is some dream that on the deck,
                You've fallen cold and dead.
My Captain does not answer, his lips are pale and still;
My father does not feel my arm, he has no pulse nor will;
The ship is anchored safe and sound, its voyage closed and done;
From fearful trip, the victor ship comes in with object won:
    Exult, O shores, and ring, O bells!
        But I, with mournful tread,
            Walk the deck my Captain lies,
                Fallen cold and dead.

WALT WHITMAN

Nancy Hanks, from a family of pioneers who since the 1600s had been slowly making their way west from the Atlantic coast, married the illiterate carpenter-farmer Thomas Lincoln. Their son, Abraham, was born in a log cabin in the slave state of Kentucky on February 12, 1809. His boyhood was a ceaseless struggle against hardship and poverty. His mother died when he was only nine.

Nancy Hanks

If Nancy Hanks
Came back as a ghost,
Seeking news
Of what she loved most,
She'd ask first
"Where's my son?
What's happened to Abe?
What's he done?

"Poor little Abe,
Left all alone
Except for Tom,
Who's a rolling stone;
He was only nine
The year I died.
I remember still
How hard he cried.

"Scraping along
In a little shack,
With hardly a shirt
To cover his back,
And a prairie wind
To blow him down,
Or pinching times
If he went to town.

"You wouldn't know
About my son?
Did he grow tall?
Did he have fun?
Did he learn to read?
Did he get to town?
Do you know his name?
Did he get on?"

ROSEMARY CARR BENÉT

V

THE EXPANSION OF THE NATION

THE WAR THAT FREED THE SLAVES also transformed America's industrial life. It had become a nation of great enterprises. Millions of men, women, and children left their villages and farms to work in huge industrial complexes. Millions of others migrated from their homelands in southern and eastern Europe in search of peace and prosperity in America. They made up the second great wave of immigration, its peak from the 1880s to the 1920s. (A third great wave would begin in the 1960s, but more on that later.)

New York was the chief port of entry for the greatest number of immigrants. At first they were received at Castle Garden, a tiny island off the foot of Manhattan. In 1892 a new reception center on Ellis Island replaced it. Most of the immigrants were unskilled workers. Skilled or not, they all faced the constant threat of unemployment. Business cycles of ups and downs made jobs unstable when depressions occurred.

Industrialists liked to hire immigrants who were grateful for any job; they were not likely to complain about anything. Foreigners were usually paid the lowest wages and worked the longest hours, often in poor conditions that caused frequent injury. Some employers encouraged differences among the ethnic groups to discourage union organization. Nevertheless, workers often joined unions and struck for better wages and working conditions.

The children of many immigrants worked, too. Millions of child laborers were deprived of schooling to help support their families. They often held jobs where conditions were the worst and employers the most ruthless—in mines, factories, textile mills, tenement sweatshops. Their death toll was high—from overwork, malnutrition, disease, and accidents.

America suffered hard times again and again. The worst was the Great Depression of the 1930s. The country's entire economic structure collapsed in October 1929. It began a decade-long period of widespread unemployment and poverty marked as one of the greatest calamities in American history. Many millions of people—workers, farmers, native-born, immigrants, professionals, the middle class, men and women, young and old, black and white—knew pain and sorrow, loss and death. Despite difficult times, however, people took pride in the accomplishments of their young nation.

Inspired by the spectacular view from Pikes Peak in Colorado, Bates wrote this poem in 1893. Readers believed that the poem cried out for a musical setting, which was provided by the American composer Samuel A. Ward.

America the Beautiful

O beautiful for spacious skies,
    For amber waves of grain,
For purple mountain majesties
    Above the fruited plain!
      America! America!
    God shed His grace on thee
And crown thy good with brotherhood
    From sea to shining sea!

O beautiful for pilgrim feet,
    Whose stern, impassioned stress
A thoroughfare for freedom beat
    Across the wilderness!
      America! America!
    God mend thine every flaw,
Confirm thy soul in self-control,
    Thy liberty in law!

O beautiful for heroes proved
    In liberating strife,
Who more than self their country loved,
    And mercy more than life!
      America! America!
    May God thy gold refine,
Till all success be nobleness,
    And every gain divine!

O beautiful for patriot dream
    That sees beyond the years
Thine alabaster cities gleam
    Undimmed by human tears!
      America! America!
    God shed His grace on thee
And crown thy good with brotherhood
    From sea to shining sea!

KATHARINE LEE BATES

This poem was first published in 1925, when Hughes was twenty-three. The first line echoes the voice of Walt Whitman. In New York City's Harlem, where young Hughes had lived, a mood of defiance and impatience had taken hold. The great gap between the American creed and American practice was denounced by many black writers.

I, TOO

I, too, sing America.

I am the darker brother.
They send me to eat in the kitchen
When company comes,
But I laugh,
And eat well,
And grow strong.

Tomorrow,
I'll be at the table
When company comes.
Nobody'll dare
Say to me,
"Eat in the kitchen,"
Then.

Besides,
They'll see how beautiful I am
And be ashamed—

I, too, am America.

LANGSTON HUGHES

In this poem, published in 1922, Hughes uses the dialect of the streets to express a mother's point of view as she speaks nobly for all black women. It became one of his most beloved poems.

Mother to Son

Well, son, I'll tell you:
Life for me ain't been no crystal stair.
It's had tacks in it,
And splinters,
And boards torn up,
And places with no carpet on the floor—
Bare.
But all the time
I'se been a-climbin' on,
And reachin' landin's,
And turnin' corners,
And sometimes goin' in the dark
Where there ain't been no light.
So boy, don't you turn back.
Don't you set down on the steps
'Cause you finds it's kinder hard.
Don't you fall now—
For I'se still goin', honey,
I'se still climbin',
And life for me ain't been no crystal stair.

LANGSTON HUGHES

This poem was written in 1925, when Cullen was twenty-two years old, the year that Color, *his first book of poems, appeared.*

Incident

Once riding in old Baltimore,
　　Heart-filled, head-filled with glee,
I saw a Baltimorean
　　Keep looking straight at me.

Now I was eight and very small,
　　And he was no whit bigger,
And so I smiled, but he poked out
　　His tongue and called me, "Nigger."

I saw the whole of Baltimore
　　From May until December:
Of all the things that happened there
　　That's all that I remember

COUNTEE CULLEN

*S*andburg was a newspaper reporter, in and out of work at the time, when his first volume of verse, Chicago Poems, *was published in 1916. His rich imagination explored a world almost wholly ignored in poetry. In "Chicago," readers can see the power and ugliness of the great American city.*

Chicago

Hog Butcher for the World,
Tool Maker, Stacker of Wheat,
Player with Railroads and the Nation's Freight Handler;
Stormy, husky, brawling,
City of the Big Shoulders:

They tell me you are wicked and I believe them, for I have seen your
    painted women under the gas lamps luring the farm boys.
And they tell me you are crooked and I answer: Yes, it is true I have
    seen the gunman kill and go free to kill again.
And they tell me you are brutal and my reply is: On the faces of women
    and children I have seen the marks of wanton hunger.
And having answered so I turn once more to those who sneer at this my
    city, and I give them back the sneer and say to them:
Come and show me another city with lifted head singing so proud to
    be alive and coarse and strong and cunning.
Flinging magnetic curses amid the toil of piling job on job, here is a
    tall bold slugger set vivid against the little soft cities;
Fierce as a dog with tongue lapping for action, cunning as a savage
    pitted against the wilderness,

Bareheaded,
Shoveling,
Wrecking,
Planning,
Building, breaking, rebuilding,
Under the smoke, dust all over his mouth, laughing with white teeth,
Under the terrible burden of destiny laughing as a young man laughs,
Laughing even as an ignorant fighter laughs who has never lost a battle,
Bragging and laughing that under his wrist is the pulse, and under his
    ribs the heart of the people,
               Laughing!
Laughing the stormy, husky, brawling laughter of Youth, half-naked,
    sweating, proud to be Hog Butcher, Tool Maker, Stacker of
    Wheat, Player with Railroads and Freight Handler to the Nation.

CARL SANDBURG

Lazarus's sonnet was commissioned for the Statue of Liberty in 1883 and is engraved on the statue's pedestal.

The New Colossus

Not like the brazen giant of Greek fame,
With conquering limbs astride from land to land;
Here at our sea-washed, sunset gates shall stand
A mighty woman with a torch, whose flame
Is the imprisoned lightning, and her name
Mother of Exiles. From her beacon-hand
Glows world-wide welcome; her mild eyes command
The air-bridged harbor that twin cities frame.
"Keep, ancient lands, your storied pomp!" cries she
With silent lips. "Give me your tired, your poor,
Your huddled masses yearning to breathe free,
The wretched refuse of your teeming shore.
Send these, the homeless, tempest-tost to me—
I lift my lamp beside the golden door!"

EMMA LAZARUS

On January 12, 1912, in Lawrence, Massachusetts, the biggest textile town in the world at the time, thousands of workers poured into the streets and onto the picket lines when employers cut their wages. Workers, already at the starvation point, shouted, "Better to starve fighting than to starve working." Most of the mill hands were immigrants. After ten weeks on strike, they won a 10 percent wage increase. Perhaps the best expression of that experience is the poem "Bread and Roses." It was written by Oppenheim when he saw young girls picketing with a banner that read We Want Bread, and Roses, Too.

Bread and Roses

As we come marching, marching in the beauty
    of the day,
A million darkened kitchens, a thousand mill
    lofts gray,
Are touched with all the radiance that a sudden
    sun discloses,
For the people hear us singing: "Bread and
    roses! Bread and roses!"

As we come marching, marching, we battle too
    for men,
For they are women's children, and we mother
    them again.
Our lives shall not be sweated from birth until
    life closes;
Hearts starve as well as bodies; give us bread,
    but give us roses!

As we come marching, marching, unnumbered
    women dead
Go crying through our singing their ancient
    cry for bread.
Small art and love and beauty their drudging
    spirits knew.
Yes, it is bread we fight for—but we fight for
    roses, too!

As we come marching, marching, we bring the
    greater days.
The rising of the women means the rising of
    the race.
No more the drudge and idler—ten that toil
    where one reposes,
But a sharing of life's glories: Bread and roses!
    Bread and roses!

JAMES OPPENHEIM

This quatrain protesting child labor hit home so powerfully it quickly became famous. Children worked at all kinds of jobs—from making artificial flowers in tenement flats to sorting coal in the mines or tending rows of machines in huge factories. In South Carolina's mills, kids five, six, and seven years old worked long hours for forty cents a day. In Pennsylvania's silk mills, thousands of girls under sixteen years of age worked from 6:30 at night until 6:30 the next morning.

Golf Links

The golf links lie so near the mill
    That almost every day
The laboring children can look out
    And see the men at play.

SARAH N. CLEGHORN

The poet, long an ardent opponent of slavery and racism, also wrote for working men and women who believed in resisting oppression in whatever form it took.

Poem

In the earnest path of duty,
  With the high hopes and hearts sincere,
We, to useful lives aspiring,
  Daily meet to labor here.

No vain dreams of earthly glory
  Urge us onward to explore
Far-extending realms of knowledge,
  With their rich and varied store;

But, with hope of aiding others,
  Gladly we perform our part;
Nor forget, the mind, while storing,
  We must educate the heart,—

Teach it hatred of oppression,
  Truest love of God and man;
Thus our high and holy calling
  May accomplish His great plan.

Not the great and gifted only
  He appoints to do his will,
But each one, however lowly,
  Has a mission to fulfill.

Knowing this, toil we unwearied,
  With true hearts and purpose high;—
We would win a wreath immortal
  Whose bright flowers ne'er fade and die.

CHARLOTTE L. FORTEN GRIMKÉ

The 1930s were the years of America's Great Depression. As businesses collapsed, banks failed, and factories closed, millions of families lost their livelihood. The poet was born just as the U.S. stock market crashed and hard times began.

Depression

We heard people were standing
In bread lines in town.
Everywhere people were begging for work
And nothing much to be found,
That much we knew.
        But we were fine,
        My sister and I,
There on our grandmother's place.

Living in the tenant's house,
Three rooms on a pasture hill,
We had the grass, the trees,
        Fresh air, the sky,
        And all those animals.

We had a father who liked to farm
And a mother who built a bookcase,
Then filled it with books and dreams.

People were begging for work . . .
Were standing in lines for food.
It was a terrible time for many,
But we had everything, my sister and I.
We were growing up rich.

ISABEL JOSHLIN GLASER

This chant, which rose from an anonymous voice, told of the deep trouble farm folks were facing during the Great Depression. Only when President Franklin D. Roosevelt took office in 1933 was any legislation passed to help the farmers.

Seven-Cent Cotton and Forty-Cent Meat

Seven-cent cotton and forty-cent meat,
How in the world can a poor man eat?
Flour up high and cotton down low,
How in the world can we raise the dough?
Clothes worn out, shoes run down,
Old slouch hat with a hole in the crown.
Back nearly broken and fingers all sore,
Cotton gone down to rise no more.

Seven-cent cotton and eight-dollar pants,
Who in the world has got a chance?
We can't buy clothes and we can't buy meat;
Too much cotton and not enough to eat.
Can't help each other, what shall we do?
I can't explain it so it's up to you.
Seven-cent cotton and two-dollar hose,
Guess we'll have to do without any clothes.

Seven-cent cotton and forty-cent meat,
How in the world can a poor man eat?
Mules in the barn, no crops laid by,
Corn crib empty and the cow's gone dry.
Well water low, nearly out of sight,
Can't take a bath on Saturday night.
No use talking, any man is beat
With seven-cent cotton and forty-cent meat.

Seven-cent cotton and forty-cent meat,
How in the world can a poor man eat?
Poor getting poorer all around here;
Kids coming regular every year.
Fatten our hogs, take 'em to town,
All we get is six cents a pound.
Very next day we have to buy it back,
Forty cents a pound in a paper sack.

We'll raise our cotton, we'll raise our meat.
We'll raise everything we eat.
We'll raise our chickens, pigs, and corn;
We'll make a living just as sure as you're born.
Farmers getting stronger every year,
Babies getting fatter all around here.
No use talking, Roosevelt's the man,
To show the world that the farmer can.

Anonymous

VI
WARS

❖◆❖

AMERICA'S HISTORY HAS BEEN RATHER SHORT,
compared with that of many other countries. Yet our nation has been
drawn into seven officially declared wars. The American Revolution—the
war for independence from Great Britain—was followed by the War of
1812 (again with Britain), the Mexican War, the Civil War, the Spanish-
American War of 1898, and then World War I (1914–1918), called "the
war to end all wars." (It was not, of course.) On December 7, 1941, when
Japanese planes struck Pearl Harbor, World War II began, with the United
States entering the struggle to defeat the Axis powers—Germany and
Japan. And without the approval of Congress (required by the
Constitution), armed forces have been sent beyond our borders more than
160 times.

Nearly three hundred thousand Americans died in World War II, and
more than twice that number were wounded. Other nations lost far more.
The bombing of civilian populations in Germany and Japan took huge
tolls during the war, which climaxed with the dropping of atomic bombs
on Hiroshima and Nagasaki.

Near the war's end, the world learned of the systematic murder of six
million Jews in the Holocaust under Germany's Adolf Hitler. But the
racism igniting the Holocaust was not limited to the Nazis. In the United
States, the president's Executive Order 9066 forced all Americans of
Japanese descent into relocation camps. During the war, the armed forces
were segregated, and discrimination was evident in the war industries.

Whatever the war, poets did their share of the fighting. Some, however,
joined with other citizens—conscientious objectors—to protest war and
uphold their conviction that peaceful solutions to conflicts between or
within nations are possible. By saying no to war, they acted out of the
deep belief that killing is wrong no matter what the circumstances.

Whatever choice poets made—to fight or to resist war—their experi-
ences are reflected in some of the poems that follow.

Any review of the media during wartime will show how these outlets are used to instill hatred—often racist in tone—of whoever the enemy happens to be.

———◆———

The Last Good War—and Afterward

We saved enough tinfoil
To wrap the entire world,
Said the Pledge of Allegiance,
Read a chapter of the Bible each day,
And even prayed . . . at school.
Then we turned our radios on,
Went to the movies . . . saw newsreels
    And learned to hate
    Whole nations of people
    We would have to learn
    To love again, later.

ISABEL JOSHLIN GLASER

Living through several wars led Kemp to this ironic view of the hullabaloo that so often accompanies the call to arms.

———◆———

I Sing the Battle

I sing the song of the great clean guns that belch forth death at will.
Ah, but the wailing mothers, the lifeless forms and still!

I sing the songs of the billowing flags, the bugles that cry before.
Ah, but the skeletons flapping rags, the lips that speak no more!

I sing the clash of bayonets and sabres that flash and cleave.
And wilt thou sing the maimed ones, too, that go with pinned-up sleeve?

I sing acclaimed generals that bring the victory home.
Ah, but the broken bodies that drip like honey-comb!

I sing the hearts triumphant, long ranks of marching men.
And wilt thou sing the shadowy hosts that never march again?

HARRY KEMP

Millay speaks for those who have resisted the call to violent action throughout our history, from colonial time through today. Conscientious objectors risked reputation, livelihood, and life itself to raise their voices against war and violence.

>◆<

Conscientious Objector

I shall die, but that is all that I shall do for Death.

I hear him leading his horse out of the stall; I hear the clatter on the barn floor.
He is in haste; he has business in Cuba, business in the Balkans,
    many calls to make this morning.
But I will not hold the bridle while he cinches the girth.
And he may mount by himself: I will not give him a leg up.

Though he flick my shoulders with his whip, I will not tell him which way the fox ran.
With his hoof on my breast, I will not tell him where the black boy hides in the swamp.
I shall die, but that is all that I shall do for Death; I am not on his payroll.

I will not tell him the whereabouts of my friends nor of my enemies either.
Though he promise me much, I will not map him the route to any man's door.
Am I a spy in the land of the living, that I should deliver men to Death?
Brother, the password and the plans of our city are safe with me; never through me
Shall you be overcome.

EDNA ST. VINCENT MILLAY

The poet imagines what American children were trained to do when the Japanese attack on Pearl Harbor in 1941 plunged the United States into war. Poet Fell was born two years after that war ended.

Basic Training

In the kitchen my mother is cooking.
We are watching World War Two
in the living room. A voice says
Pearl Harbor has just been attacked.
My mother's cry, a broken plate.

When the alarm rings, we march
into the school basement where it's safer.
If there isn't time,
crouch under a desk for protection
from atom bombs.

We practice jungle belly crawl
through the high grass in Gordon's yard,
Red Ryder air rifles cradled in our elbows.
For sneaking up on enemies, walk
heel first, then the whole foot, quietly.

Take a bottle cap. Gouge out
the cork heart. Put it inside your shirt
over your own heart, the cap outside.
Push them back together:
a war medal.

Heroes limp from battle
at Park Theater, an eye out
for enemies in the dark aisles.
Near the candy stand, a secret nod to the clerk.
She knows who we are.

On every street corner, granite markers
named for soldiers.
They have come home
to squat forever, like the rest of us,
on the curbstones.

MARY FELL

Early in 1942, soon after the attack on Pearl Harbor, President Franklin D. Roosevelt signed Executive Order 9066, allowing armed forces commanders to set up military zones with the authority to remove anyone from these areas, regardless of race, nationality, or age. On March 1, the head of the Western Defense Command announced that all persons of Japanese ancestry would have to leave the Pacific Coast military area. No individual charges were placed against any of the 110,000 men, women, and children, two-thirds of whom were native-born Americans with full citizenship rights. But they were forced to move into large internment camps in isolated inland areas. The poet imagines what it was like for the young people who went through this unjust and humiliating experience.

In Response to Executive Order 9066:

All Americans of Japanese Descent Must Report to Relocation Centers

Dear Sirs:
Of course I'll come. I've packed my galoshes
and three packets of tomato seeds. Denise calls them
love apples. My father says where we're going
they won't grow.

I am a fourteen-year-old girl with bad spelling
and a messy room. If it helps any, I will tell you
I have always felt funny using chopsticks
and my favorite food is hot dogs.
My best friend is a white girl named Denise—
we look at boys together. She sat in front of me
all through grade school because of our names:
O'Connor, Ozawa. I know the back of Denise's head very well.

I tell her she's going bald. She tells me I copy on tests.
We're best friends.

I saw Denise today in Geography class.
She was sitting on the other side of the room.
"You're trying to start a war," she said, "giving secrets
away to the Enemy, Why can't you keep your big
mouth shut?"

I didn't know what to say.
I gave her a packet of tomato seeds
and asked her to plant them for me, told her
when the first tomato ripened
she'd miss me.

DWIGHT OKITA

When Nazi dictator Adolf Hitler forced millions of Jews and other religious and political groups into his death camps during World War II, each person was assigned a number that was tattooed on his or her forearm. Sometimes a great gulf separated concentration-camp survivors from their children.

Tattoo

My father won't talk about the numbers
3-7-8-2-5 between the wrist and elbow
blue as blood on his left forearm
Instead, he spreads himself over me
spilling his protection, like acid, until it burns
I wear him like a cloak, sweat under the weight

There were stories in the lines on his face
the nervous blue flash in his eyes
his bone-crushing hugs
I am drowning in his silence
trying to stay afloat on curiosity
Questions choke me and I swallow hard

We don't breathe the same air
speak the same language
live in the same universe
We are continents, worlds apart
I am sorry my life has remained unscathed
His scars still bleed, his bruises don't fade

If I could trade places with him
I would pad the rest of his days
wrap him in gauze and velvet
absorb the shocks and treat his wounds
I would scrub the numbers from his flesh
extinguish the fire and give him back his life

GREGG SHAPIRO

With a play on monuments to the Unknown Soldier, Auden takes an ironic view of the "average" man.

The Unknown Citizen

(To JS/07/M378
This Marble Monument Is Erected by the State)

He was found by the Bureau of Statistics to be
One against whom there was no official complaint,
And all the reports on his conduct agree
That, in the modern sense of an old-fashioned word, he was a saint,
For in everything he did he served the Greater Community.
Except for the War till the day he retired
He worked in a factory and never got fired,
But satisfied his employers, Fudge Motors Inc.
Yet he wasn't a scab or odd in his views,
For his Union reports that he paid his dues,
(Our report on his Union shows it was sound)
And our Social Psychology workers found
That he was popular with his mates and liked a drink.
The Press are convinced that he bought a paper every day
And that his reactions to advertisements were normal in every way.
Policies taken out in his name prove that he was fully insured,
And his Health-card shows he was once in hospital but left it cured.
Both Producers Research and High-Grade Living declare
He was fully sensible to the advantages of the Installment Plan
And had everything necessary to the Modern Man,
A phonograph, a radio, a car and a frigidaire.
Our researchers into Public Opinion are content
That he held the proper opinions for the time of year:
When there was peace, he was for peace; when there was war, he went.
He was married and added five children to the population,
Which our Eugenist says was the right number for a parent of his generation.
And our teachers report that he never interfered with their education.
Was he free? Was he happy? The question is absurd:
Had anything been wrong, we should certainly have heard.

W. H. AUDEN

VII

CHANGING AMERICA

T HE LAST HALF OF THE TWENTIETH CENTURY
and the beginning of the twenty-first century did not lack for great events
or trends to dominate the news. The struggle for civil rights, always a force
but accelerating powerfully in the 1950s, shook the nation, North as well
as South. More foreign wars were fought: in Korea (1950–1953); in
Vietnam—an agonizingly long conflict that stretched from 1965 to 1973;
the brief Gulf War of 1990–1991. Near the end of the 1960s, another
great wave of immigration began, bringing at least thirty million people to
America by the opening of the twenty-first century.

When World War II ended in 1945, black veterans came home deter-
mined to achieve racial equality. The United States, calling itself "the
leader of the free world" in its Cold War with the Soviet Union, did not
completely allow the black community to obtain equal citizenship or
equal opportunity.

With the struggle for full freedom underway, blacks and their allies
sought three rights: integrated public schools, desegregation of public
accommodations, and, perhaps most important, voting rights. In 1954 the
Supreme Court ruled that school segregation was unconstitutional.
Millions rejoiced that at last, more than ninety years after emancipation,
basic civil rights for all were recognized. Violent resistance to the court's
ruling mounted rapidly in the South. Under the leadership of Dr. Martin
Luther King Jr. and others, step by painful step civil rights groups made

progress in wiping out discrimination in the schools, the workplace, the ballot box, and the community. Local, state, and federal government institutions were gradually reshaped. Prejudice, poverty, failing schools, separation between races and cultures, and a widening gap between rich and poor still prevailed to some degree as the new century began.

The millions migrating to the United States since the 1960s have come from all parts of the world. Like those who entered before them, they moved from their homelands to America out of the simple desire for a better life. The rich mixture of immigrants can be seen in the example of just one elementary school of about nine hundred students in New York City. There, the children speak thirty-six different languages.

The majority of new immigrants have come from Latin America and Asia. They are welcomed by dozens of industries in need of their labor power. The newcomers work in factories, on farms, in hotels and restaurants, in construction, and many other places. It is clear that American enterprises depend on immigrant labor.

That their labor is badly needed doesn't mean that everyone welcomes them. The same heated debate over immigration policy has gone on throughout our history. For the newcomers, dreams often lead to disappointment. Life can be difficult and painful, and some return to their birthplace. Still, many build a new life and open doors of greater opportunity for their children.

American involvement in the Vietnam War began in 1950 and kept expanding under Presidents Eisenhower, Kennedy, Johnson, and Nixon. The United States finally withdrew in 1973, after fifty-eight thousand Americans had lost their lives.

Ode for the American Dead in Asia

God love you now, if no one else will ever,
Corpse in the paddy, or dead on a high hill
In the fine and ruinous summer of a war
You never wanted. All your false flags were
Of bravery and ignorance, like grade school maps:
Colors of countries you would never see—
Until that weekend in eternity
When, laughing, well armed, perfectly ready to kill
The world and your brother, the safe commanders sent
You into your future. Oh, dead on a hill,
Dead in a paddy, leeched and tumbled to
A tomb of footnotes. We mourn a changeling: you:
Handselled to poverty and drummed to war
By distinguished masters whom you never knew.

THOMAS MCGRATH

This poem is written from the viewpoint of the two million Vietnamese who died in the Vietnam War.

What Were They Like?

1) Did the people of Vietnam
   use lanterns of stone?
2) Did they hold ceremonies
   to reverence the opening of buds?
3) Were they inclined to quiet laughter?
4) Did they use bone and ivory,
   jade and silver, for ornament?
5) Had they an epic poem?
6) Did they distinguish between speech and singing?

1) Sir, their light hearts turned to stone.
   It is not remembered whether in gardens
   stone lanterns illumined pleasant ways.
2) Perhaps they gathered once to delight in blossom,
   but after the children were killed
   there were no more buds.
3) Sir, laughter is bitter to the burned mouth.
4) A dream ago, perhaps. Ornament is for joy.
   All the bones were charred.
5) It is not remembered. Remember,
   most were peasants; their life
   was in rice and bamboo.
   When peaceful clouds were reflected in the paddies
   and the water buffalo stepped surely along terraces,
   maybe fathers told their sons old tales.
   When bombs smashed those mirrors
   there was time only to scream.
6) There is an echo yet
   of their speech which was like a song.
   It was reported their singing resembled
   the flight of moths in moonlight.
   Who can say? It is silent now.

DENISE LEVERTOV

The Reverend Dr. Martin Luther King Jr., young pastor of a church in Montgomery, Alabama, became the leader of a city-bus boycott in 1955. It ended in victory fifty-five weeks later, when Montgomery agreed to desegregate its bus system. He was awarded the Nobel Peace Prize in 1964 in recognition of his nonviolence precept that guided the nationwide civil rights movement. He was assassinated in Memphis, Tennessee, in 1968.

Martin Luther King

Because he took a stand for peace
and dreamed that he would find
a way to spread equality
to all of humankind,

Because he hated violence
and fought with words, not guns,
he won a timely victory
as one of freedom's sons;

Because he died for liberty,
the bells of history ring
to honor the accomplishments
of Martin Luther King.

AILEEN FISHER

In 1965 Malcolm X was killed by an assassin. He had been a leader of the Black Muslim movement, which believed that hard work, efficiency, and self-sacrifice could mean a better life, on terms that stressed separation of the races rather than integration. His autobiography greatly influenced the thinking of a huge audience, both black and white.

For Malcolm, a Year After

Compose for Red a proper verse;
Adhere to foot and strict iamb;
Control the burst of angry words
Or they might boil and break the dam.
Or they might boil and overflow
And drench me, drown me, drive me mad.
So swear no oath, so shed no tear,
And sing no song blue Baptist sad.
Evoke no image, stir no flame,
And spin no yarn across the air.
Make empty anglo tea lace words—
Make them dead white and dry bone bare.

Compose a verse for Malcolm man,
And make it rime and make it prim.
The verse will die—as all men do—
But not the memory of him!
Death might come singing sweet like C,
Or knocking like the old folk say,
The moon and stars may pass away,
But not the anger of that day.

ETHERIDGE KNIGHT

Despite overwhelming poverty on many Indian reservations, Native Americans take pride in their heritage.

The Reservation

You seldom talked about the Indian side
of the family, a thing of shame
after World War II, when the men came home, victorious,
the women herded back to houses isolated
as reservations. I can still see you
in an organdy apron, your black hair iridescent,
nearly blue as indigo bunting feathers
drawing down sunlight—how you tortured
that wild hair, and mine, each night with the stern
jabs of bobby pins into tight curls, attempting
tameness. "Be a lady," you said, "lower your voice,
sit with your knees together," as if you wanted
to pin my entire body into a single knot.
But nothing held. At the first hint of rain
your hair fell out soft and long to your shoulders
tired from pushing clothes through the old ringer washer,
stretching your still young flesh up towards the clothesline
where you hung your children's shirts and dresses,
ghosts flapping free from the small bodies
that clung to you all through the 'fifties.
You jerked the clothesline forward into empty air.
Sometimes after supper, when you washed dishes, I dried, you slipped
into storytelling, telling me about your Blackfoot father,
so handsome he should have been on the nickel,
shooting dice, shooting pistols in the air
that time he chose to ride a stolen horse
through town in love battle for his wife.
Did you know your words led me into a secret life
away from yours, I, "the savage," crawling around
in bushes, hiding out with birds, my hands
hugging the dark earth while other children
played silly games in the schoolyard?

Years later you told me you were a tomboy as a child.
How I loved you for that, your own secret life,
remembering the crying spells you had every spring
when you would take off your stiff apron, take me
by my dirt-blessed hand deep into the woods behind the house
where we sat in silence, mother and daughter,
among spring beauties and curled adder's tongue.

SUSAN CLEMENTS

Life can be tough on the Indian reservation, the one-time home of the poet at Pine Ridge, South Dakota.

Petroglyphs of Serena

And then it was winter again.
Oh, man, a desperate Dakota winter.
Our neighbors shot a starving deer
behind their HUD house
and butchered it in their front yard.
They wrapped large pieces in Hefty bags
and stored them in the trunk
of their broken-down '72 Olds.
In February they ran out of wood so they
burned chunks of old tires in the woodstove.
Their children went to school smudged
and smelling like burnt rubber.
A typical hard-ass Dakota winter.
All across the Rez, wild Indians
shiver-danced around woodstoves
and howled the most wondrous songs
of brilliant poverty.

ADRIAN C. LOUIS

America has been peopled with immigrants ever since the first group walked across the land bridge from Siberia to Alaska some forty thousand years ago. Throughout the span of American history, historians have recorded three waves of migration: from the colonial time of the 1600s to about 1800; from the 1820s to the 1920s; and today, beginning in the late 1960s, when immigration laws became more liberal, and continuing to this day. These new immigrants are mostly Asian and Hispanic, compelled to leave their homelands by poor social or economic conditions. At least thirty million people have come here in this latest wave. They, like every newcomer, hope to integrate into the mainstream of our society.

Immigrants in Our Own Land

We are born with dreams in our hearts,
looking for better days ahead.
At the gates we are given new papers,
our old clothes arc takcn
and we are given overalls like mechanics wear.
We are given shots and doctors ask questions.
Then we gather in another room
where counselors orient us to the new land
we will now live in. We take tests.
Some of us were craftsmen in the old world,
good with our hands and proud of our work.
Others were good with their heads.
They used common sense like scholars
use glasses and books to reach the world.
But most of us didn't finish high school.

The old men who have lived here stare at us,
from deep disturbed eyes, sulking, retreated.
We pass them as they stand around idle,
leaning on shovels and rakes or against walls.
Our expectations are high: in the old world,
they talked about rehabilitation,
about being able to finish school,
and learning an extra good trade.
But right away we are sent to work as dishwashers,
to work in fields for three cents an hour.
The administration says this is temporary
so we go about our business, blacks with blacks,
poor whites with poor whites,
chicanos and indians by themselves.
The administration says this is right,
no mixing of cultures, let them stay apart,
like in the old neighborhoods we came from.

We came here to get away from false promises,
from dictators in our neighborhoods,
who wore blue suits and broke our doors down
when they wanted, arrested us when they felt like,
swinging clubs and shooting guns as they pleased.
But it's no different here. It's all concentrated.
The doctors don't care, our bodies decay,
our minds deteriorate, we learn nothing of value.
Our lives don't get better, we go down quick.

My cell is crisscrossed with laundry lines,
my T-shirts, boxer shorts, socks and pants are drying.
Just like it used to be in my neighborhood:
from all the tenements laundry hung window to window.
Across the way Joey is sticking his hands
through the bars to hand Felipe a cigarette,
men are hollering back and forth cell to cell,
saying their sinks don't work,
or somebody downstairs hollers angrily
about a toilet overflowing,
or that the heaters don't work.

I ask Coyote next door to shoot me over
a little more soap to finish my laundry.
I look down and see new immigrants coming in,
mattresses rolled up and on their shoulders,
new haircuts and brogan boots,
looking around, each with a dream in his heart,
thinking he'll get a chance to change his life.

But in the end, some will just sit around
talking about how good the old world was.
Some of the younger ones will become gangsters.
Some will die and others will go on living
without a soul, a future, or a reason to live.
Some will make it out of here with hate in their eyes,
but so very few make it out of here as human
as they came in, they leave wondering what good they are now
as they look at their hands so long away from their tools,
as they look at themselves, so long gone from their families,
so long gone from life itself, so many things have changed.

JIMMY SANTIAGO BACA

*T*he poet's work reflects her deep commitment as a social activist, striving to make life better for the many who lack privilege and power.

Occupant: Blue Roof Apartments

The mail addressed to Occupant
wants to bury me cheap,
wants to sell me a family album
or *Funk and Wagnall's Encyclopedia*
on the installment plan.
Not one letter offers what I want
or need: a set of retread tires,
a gold crown for that top left molar,
that 49ers jacket my son saw at the mall.
Their surveys don't show
that plopped beneath
our blue-roofed apartments
we are all on welfare
or navy enlistees.
Our cobalt blue roofs flash
    Here we are,
    the anonymous poor
a sea of misery stored
in the city's largest housing complex.
The apartments next door
with understated brown roofs,
security guard and pool
is where we'll move
when we get the next job,
the next raise,
the next big promotion,
that next step up
that guarantees us mail
addressed to us by name.

DIANA GARCÍA

Mora, herself of Hispanic descent, knows of the gap between parents born in another country, another culture, and their children growing up in a strange America.

Elena

My Spanish isn't enough.
I remember how I'd smile
listening to my little ones,
understanding every word they'd say,
their jokes, their songs, their plots.
      Vamos a pedirle dulces a mamá. Vamos.
But that was in Mexico.
Now my children go to American high schools.
They speak English. At night they sit around
the kitchen table, laugh with one another.
I stand by the stove and feel dumb, alone.
I bought a book to learn English.
My husband frowned, drank more beer.
My oldest said, "*Mamá*, he doesn't want you
to be smarter than he is." I'm forty,
embarrassed at mispronouncing words,
embarrassed at the laughter of my children,
the grocer, the mailman. Sometimes I take
my English book and lock myself in the bathroom,
say the thick words softly,
for if I stop trying, I will be deaf
when my children need my help.

PAT MORA

*T*he poet comments on what has lately been called racial profiling, that is, predicting patterns of behavior by the way people look—their skin color, facial appearance, or other physical feature.

Enemies

We watch
        TV

and see
        enemies fighting.

Close-ups of
                narrow faces
                deep dark eyes
                full young lips.

There are
        two.

Which is an Arab?

        Which is a Jew?

CHARLOTTE ZOLOTOW

Although written in the twentieth century, when rockets were among the many weapons of modern war and violent conflict that devastated families and nations, the poem voices the fears of all mothers at any time in history.

War

Every time I look
they are running down the road,
the man holding the wrist
of the young girl, her feet
bare in the dust, her head
flung back as if
she were running beyond
endurance. The other man runs
with his mouth shouting anguish,
a baby held to one shoulder,
a dark haired boy clasped
against his chest, legs dangling
to his father's knees.

The caption says they are fleeing
rockets, that the man holds
the bodies of his two children.
For days they keep running
    as my tears fall.

One day I wonder how
the photographer knew
those children were dead?
That man could be running
to save them, his face
opened by fear.
But both men
wear grief, as if death
not only falls in the distance,
but runs beside them.

I hold this piece of newsprint, half
a world's rotation
from that dusty road.
If the knowledge of this man
clasping his lost sweetness
is unbearable to me, how
will he ever stop running, how
will he ever
hold their mother
with tender eyes?

I keep the picture
in a drawer. If it were pinned
to the wall, I would grow
a stone heart.

AMY MCARTHUR

Afterword

Where?

Where after all do human rights begin?
In small places close to home
 Such are the places
Where every man, woman and child
 Seeks equal justice
 Equal opportunity
 Equal dignity

ELEANOR ROOSEVELT

Biographical Notes on Poets

W. H. AUDEN (1907–1973) was born in York, England, and educated at Oxford. Auden wrote poems that varied in subject matter from politics to modern psychology to Christianity. In 1939 he emigrated to the United States and became a citizen. He frequently lived abroad for long periods of time—in China, Germany, Spain, Italy, and Austria. In addition to publishing several volumes of poetry, he was a coauthor of the libretto for composer Igor Stravinsky's opera *The Rake's Progress.*

JIMMY SANTIAGO BACA (b. 1952), born in Santa Fe, New Mexico, is the author of several books of poetry. He won the 1988 American Book Award for *Martin and Meditations on the South Valley.*

KATHARINE LEE BATES (1859–1929), a native of Falmouth, Massachusetts, was educated at Wellesley College, where she taught English literature for forty years. Bates was made a full professor in 1891, one of the few women in the United States to hold that rank at that time.

ROSEMARY CARR BENÉT (1898–1962), born in Chicago, Illinois, was working as a journalist in France in the 1920s when she met and married Stephen Vincent Benét. They often joined their writing talents, especially in producing stories for children about events in the American past.

STEPHEN VINCENT BENÉT (1898–1943) wrote several collections of verse, in addition to the epic poem *John Brown's Body,* a Pulitzer Prize winner. Some of his poems were written together with his wife, Rosemary Carr Benét. He was born in Bethlehem, Pennsylvania.

WILLIAM CULLEN BRYANT (1794–1878), born in Cummington, Massachusetts, wrote nature poems that were published while he was still a teenager. With a reputation as a poet and critic, he moved to New York City and, as editor of the *New York Evening Post,* was an ardent defender of human rights. Late in life his blank-verse translations of the *Iliad* and the *Odyssey* were published.

SARAH N. CLEGHORN (1876–1959), born in Vermont, wrote poems about New England, mystical questions, and social issues.

SUSAN CLEMENTS (b. 1950) is of Blackfeet, Mohawk, Seneca, and European heritage and has published several books with Native American themes. She was born in Livingston Manor, New York.

ROBERT P. TRISTRAM COFFIN (1892–1955) drew upon his early years in his hometown of Brunswick, Maine, for many of his poems as well as his novels. His collection, *Strange Holiness,* won the Pulitzer Prize for poetry in 1936.

COUNTEE CULLEN (1903–1946) was born in New York City and was raised in a Methodist parsonage. He was educated in public schools and earned degrees from New York University and Harvard University. A major writer of the Harlem Renaissance, he patterned his poetry on the style of John Keats. He wrote several volumes of verse, as well as fiction, dealing with race and other issues.

RITA DOVE (b. 1952), in 1987, was the second African American to win a Pulitzer Prize in poetry. From 1993 through 1995 she served as Poet Laureate of the United States. A native of Akron, Ohio, she has written fiction as well as poetry.

PAUL LAURENCE DUNBAR (1872–1906) was born in Dayton, Ohio, to parents who had been slaves. His father had escaped to freedom and fought in the Civil War. Dunbar's first book of poems was published when he was twenty-one years old and working as an elevator operator. He popularized black literature by giving public readings. His prodigious output includes seven volumes of verse, four novels, four collections of short stories, numerous magazine articles, song lyrics, and musical plays.

RALPH WALDO EMERSON (1803–1882), as poet, philosopher, essayist, and lecturer, was one of the leading lights of nineteenth-century literature. A native of Boston, Massachusetts, he settled in Concord, Massachusetts, the writing home of such notables as Henry David Thoreau, Nathaniel Hawthorne, Margaret Fuller, and Louisa May Alcott. He wrote poems throughout his life.

MARY FELL (b. 1947), born in Worcester, Massachusetts, earned a graduate degree in fine arts at the University of Massachusetts after several years as a social worker. She teaches English at Indiana University. Her working-class background is sensed in her poems.

AILEEN FISHER (1906–2002), born in the Upper Peninsula of Michigan, was educated at the University of Chicago and the University of Missouri. Since the early 1930s, her many volumes of poetry, fiction, and nonfiction have reached untold numbers of young readers and earned many awards.

PHILIP FRENEAU (1752–1832), although coming from a wealthy merchant family, became one of the great rebels of his time. He wrote his first poems while attending Princeton University as the American Revolution broke out, and he continued to advance democratic principles long after the United States had won its independence. Born in New York City, he was looked upon as the chief poet-propagandist of the Revolution.

DIANA GARCÍA (b. 1950) was born in a migrant labor camp in California's San Joaquin Valley. She has taught creative writing at universities in Connecticut and Germany and currently teaches at California State University at Monterey Bay.

WILLIAM LLOYD GARRISON (1805–1879) was born in Newburyport, Massachusetts, of forebears who came to America as indentured servants. An apprentice printer with a passion for reading, he became the country's foremost political agitator and abolitionist. He wrote passionate editorials for his antislavery newspaper, *The Liberator,* and many poems about love as well as politics.

ISABEL JOSHLIN GLASER (b. 1929) is a native of Birmingham, Alabama, and now lives in Memphis, Tennessee. A graduate of Vanderbilt University, she has taught both high school and elementary school students. In addition to poetry, she has written short stories, articles, and reviews.

CHARLOTTE L. FORTEN GRIMKÉ
(1837–1914) was born a free black in
Philadelphia and moved to Salem, Massachusetts,
where she was an active abolitionist. During
Reconstruction, she taught the newly freed people
on St. Helena Island, South Carolina. She later
moved to Washington, D.C., where with voice and
pen she continued the struggle for racial equality.

FRANCES ELLEN WATKINS HARPER
(1825–1911), born to free black parents in
Baltimore, Maryland, became a teacher and moved
to Philadelphia, where she lectured and fought for
education, civil rights, and children's rights. She
wrote essays, fiction, and several volumes of poetry.

OLIVER WENDELL HOLMES (1809–1894)
won public fame as a poet in 1830 with "Old
Ironsides," his plea to preserve the famous warship
the *Constitution*. He was a professor of medicine
and dean of the Harvard Medical School. A
native of Cambridge, Massachusetts, he was a
popular lecturer, essayist, biographer, and
novelist, as well as a poet.

LANGSTON HUGHES (1902–1967) was born in
Joplin, Missouri, and was brought up in Lawrence,
Kansas, and Cleveland, Ohio. He worked at many
jobs in his youth, wandered around Europe and
Africa, then returned to earn a degree from
Lincoln University. Acclaimed as the Poet Laureate
of Harlem, he became one of the most productive
and popular African American writers. He wrote a
number of volumes of poetry as well as novels,
short stories, essays, plays, newspaper columns,
librettos for opera and musical comedy, stories for
children, and an autobiography. In 2002 the U.S.
Post Office issued a commemorative stamp marking
the centennial of his birth.

HARRY KEMP (1883–1960) was born in
Youngstown, Ohio, and educated at the
University of Kansas. A tramp trip around the
world and across the United States led to many
lectures as the romantic "tramp poet." While
living in New York City, he organized the Poets
Theater. His poems were published in newspapers
and books, and an autobiographical novel,
Tramping on Life, was published in 1922.

ETHERIDGE KNIGHT (1931–1991) was born
in Corinth, Mississippi, of a poor black family and
quit school at sixteen to join the army. He served
in the Korean War and, wounded in combat, fell
into drug addiction. In 1960 he was convicted of
robbery and served eight years in prison. There he
began writing narrative poetry stemming from the
black oral tradition. His first book, *Poems from
Prison*, was published a year before his release. His
books and platform readings of poetry won him
critical acclaim and honors from the Guggenheim
Foundation, the National Endowment for the Arts,
and the Poetry Society of America.

EMMA LAZARUS (1849–1887), a native of New
York City, was enraged by the grisly Russian
pogroms of the 1880s, which stimulated the mass
emigration of Jews to the United States, and
voiced her passion in many essays and poems.

DENISE LEVERTOV (1923–1997), who was
born in England, was home-schooled and began
writing very early on. Her first poem was published
when she was seventeen. During World War II,
she worked as a civilian nurse, tending to victims
of German bombings of London. When she
married an American writer, they moved to New
York City. In 1956 she became a naturalized
citizen. Departing from standard forms of verse,
she developed an open, experimental style and
soon won recognition as a leading American
poet. More than twenty volumes of her poetry
and prose were published.

ABRAHAM LINCOLN (1809–1865), born in the slave state of Kentucky of a long line of pioneers, grew up in the free state of Indiana and practiced law in Illinois. With less than a year of formal schooling, he became not only one of our greatest presidents, but one of the great masters of English prose.

ADRIAN C. LOUIS (b. 1946) is a member of the Lovelock Paiute tribe. Born and raised in Nevada, he has written several volumes of poetry.

JAMES RUSSELL LOWELL (1819–1891) was the first in an extraordinary line of family poets. He was followed by Amy Lowell, a first cousin, then great-grandnephew Robert Lowell. He was born in Cambridge, Massachusetts, wrote his first book of poems in 1841, and for some time made his living by writing. He was a teacher as well as a poet and critic, succeeding Henry Wadsworth Longfellow as a professor of modern languages at Harvard University. In his later years he was ambassador to Spain and then to Great Britain.

AMY McARTHUR (b. 1952), born in New York City, is a clinical psychologist who writes poetry and prose and also works in the graphic arts field.

THOMAS McGRATH (1916–1990) was born into an Irish-Catholic farming family in North Dakota, where he attended school. He earned a bachelor's degree at the University of North Dakota and did graduate work at Louisiana State University. Early in World War II, he worked as a shipyard welder and a labor organizer on the docks of Manhattan's West Side and then served in the military on the Aleutian Islands. The war over, he won a Rhodes scholarship to study at Oxford University. Later he taught high school and then at state universities in North Dakota and Minnesota. He served on the editorial boards of several literary journals and earned a number of fellowships.

EDNA ST. VINCENT MILLAY (1892–1950), one of the most widely read poets in the United States, was born in Rockland, Maine. Even before graduating from Vassar College, she had published a major work, "Renascence." From her love poems of the 1920s, she turned more and more to poetry that protested social injustice. She also wrote plays in verse and the libretto for the Deems Taylor opera *The King's Henchman.*

PAT MORA (b. 1942), a Chicana from El Paso, Texas, earned a master's degree from the University of Texas. As a leading figure of contemporary Hispanic poetry, she has taught at the University of New Mexico and worked as a museum director. In addition to several volumes of poetry, she has written many children's books.

DWIGHT OKITA (b. 1958), a third-generation Japanese American, is the author of *Crossing with the Light,* a book of poems. He was born and still lives in Chicago, Illinois.

JAMES OPPENHEIM (1882–1932), a native of St. Paul, Minnesota, grew up in New York City, attended Columbia University, and became a social worker and a muckraking novelist. Two volumes of his poetry were published in the early 1900s.

LAURA E. RICHARDS (1850–1943), born in Boston, Massachusetts, and a daughter of Dr. Samuel Gridley Howe and Julia Ward Howe, wrote more than eighty books, most of them for young readers. Her poems, chiefly ballads, appeared in several publications.

ELEANOR ROOSEVELT (1884–1962), born in New York City, was the niece of Theodore Roosevelt. Active in social causes, she married Franklin D. Roosevelt and, while rearing five children, continued her interest in social betterment through the years of her husband's service as governor of New York and as president of the United States. After his death, she served as U.S. delegate to the United Nations and chaired its Commission on Human Rights. She often wrote articles and essays for newspapers and magazines.

CARL SANDBURG (1878–1967) was born in Galesburg, Illinois, the son of Swedish immigrants. He put himself through college and then worked as a journalist. In 1914 his poems focused on working people's struggle to get along, as well as on historical themes. His style, like Walt Whitman's, was simple and noble. He often wrote for children and collected ballads and folk songs. His multivolume biography of Abraham Lincoln won the Pulitzer Prize.

GREGG SHAPIRO (b. 1959), born in Chicago, Illinois, is a poet and fiction writer and covers pop culture as a free-lance journalist.

LYDIA H. SIGOURNEY (1791–1865) was born in Norwich, Connecticut. Settling in Hartford, she opened a school for girls. A prolific author, she wrote some two thousand pieces for three hundred periodicals and was the author of more than fifty volumes of prose and poetry. She won huge popularity in her day. She was one of the earliest writers to address women's issues.

SAMUEL FRANCIS SMITH (1808–1895), a Baptist clergyman and poet from Boston, Massachusetts, wrote the hymn "America" in 1832 while a seminary student. It was first sung at a Fourth of July celebration in Boston that same year. The words were set to a tune that originated in Europe.

HENRY DAVID THOREAU (1817–1862) was born in Concord, Massachusetts, where he lived all his life. He brought the natural and social life of his birthplace into his literary masterpiece, *Walden.* He also wrote many essays and poems.

WALT WHITMAN (1819–1892) was born on Long Island and grew up in Brooklyn, New York. As a youth he worked as a schoolteacher, printer, and journalist. In 1855 he published *Leaves of Grass,* the first of eight ever-larger editions he would work on until his death. He helped pioneer the free-verse form of poetry and the use of everyday life of ordinary people as a subject.

JOHN GREENLEAF WHITTIER (1807–1892), a Quaker born in Massachusetts, had his first volume of poetry published at age twenty-four. He was enormously popular for his poems on rural life. He was an ardent abolitionist, never giving up the fight for full freedom for African Americans.

SAMUEL WOODWORTH (1785–1842), born in Scituate, Massachusetts, won wide popularity early on with his poem "The Old Oaken Bucket." He was a skillful writer in several fields besides poetry, working as an editor and a playwright.

CHARLOTTE ZOLOTOW (b. 1915), a native of Norfolk, Virginia, is the author of more than ninety books for children and the editor of hundreds more for her own imprint, Charlotte Zolotow Books, a part of HarperCollins Publishers. She is the recipient of the University of Minnesota's Kerlan Award for her body of work.

Acknowledgments

Every possible effort has been made to trace the ownership of each poem included in *Hour of Freedom: American History in Poetry*. If any errors or omissions have occurred, corrections will be made in subsequent printings, provided the publisher is notified of their existence.

Permission to reprint poems is gratefully acknowledged to the following:

Alfred A. Knopf for "I, Too" and "Mother to Son" from *The Collected Poems of Langston Hughes* by Langston Hughes. Copyright © 1994 by The Estate of Langston Hughes. Used by permission of Alfred A. Knopf, a division of Random House, Inc.

Arte Público Press for "Elena" by Pat Mora. Reprinted with permission from the publisher of *Chants* by Pat Mora (Houston: Arte Público Press—University of Houston, 1985).

Brandt & Hochman Literary Agents, Inc., for "Nancy Hanks" by Rosemary Benét. From *A Book of Americans* by Rosemary and Stephen Vincent Benét. Copyright © 1933 by Rosemary and Stephen Vincent Benét. Copyright renewed © 1961 by Rosemary Carr Benét; and "Peregrine White and Virginia Dare" and "Western Wagons" by Stephen Vincent Benét. From *A Book of Americans* by Rosemary and Stephen Vincent Benét. Copyright © 1933 by Rosemary and Stephen Vincent Benét. Copyright renewed © 1961 by Rosemary Carr Benét. Reprinted by permission of Brandt & Hochman Literary Agents, Inc.

Chantry Press and Susan Clements for "The Reservation" from *In the Moon Where the Deer Lose Their Horns* by Susan Clements. Copyright © 1993 by Susan Clements. Reprinted by permission of the publisher and author.

Copper Canyon Press for "Ode for the American Dead in Asia" from *Selected Poems, 1938–1988* by Thomas McGrath. Copyright © 1988 by Thomas McGrath. Reprinted with the permission of Copper Canyon Press, P.O. Box 271, Port Townsend, Washington 98368-0271.

Rita Dove for "The Abduction" from *The Yellow House on the Corner* by Rita Dove, Carnegie-Mellon University Press. Copyright © 1980 by Rita Dove. Reprinted by permission of the author.

Mary Fell for "Basic Training" from *The Persistence of Memory* by Mary Fell. Used by permission of the author.

Isabel Joshlin Glaser for "Depression" and "The Last Good War—and Afterward." Copyright © 1994. Reprinted by permission of the author, who controls all rights.

GRM Associates, Inc., for "Incident" from the book *Color* by Countee Cullen. Copyright © 1925 by Harper & Brothers. Copyright renewed © 1953 by Ida M. Cullen. Reprinted by permission of GRM Associates, Inc., Agents for the Estate of Ida M. Cullen.

Harcourt, Inc., for "Buffalo Dusk" from *Smoke and Steel* by Carl Sandburg. Copyright © 1920 by Harcourt, Inc., and renewed 1948 by Carl Sandburg; and "Chicago" from *Chicago Poems* by Carl Sandburg. Copyright © 1916 by Holt, Rinehart and Winston and renewed 1944 by Carl Sandburg; and excerpt from *The People, Yes* ("Circles") by Carl Sandburg. Copyright © 1936 by Harcourt, Inc., and renewed 1964 by Carl Sandburg; and "Washington Monument at Night" from *Slabs of the Sunburnt West* by Carl Sandburg. Copyright © 1922 by Harcourt, Inc., and renewed 1950 by Carl Sandburg. Reprinted by permission of the publisher.

Adrian C. Louis for "Petroglyphs of Serena" from *Ceremonies of the Damned* by Adrian C. Louis, published by the University of Nevada Press. Copyright © 1999 by Adrian C. Louis. Reprinted by permission of the author.

Amy McArthur for "War" by Amy McArthur. Copyright © 1995 by Amy McArthur. Reprinted by permission of the author.

New Directions Publishing Corporation for "Immigrants in Our Own Land" from *Immigrants in Our Own Land* by Jimmy Santiago Baca. Copyright © 1982 by Jimmy Santiago Baca; and "What Were They Like?" from *Poems 1960–1967* by Denise Levertov. Copyright © 1966 by Denise Levertov. Reprinted by permission of New Directions Publishing Corporation.

Dwight Okita for "In Response to Executive Order 9066: All Americans of Japanese Descent Must Report to Relocation Centers" from *Crossing with the Light* (Tia Chucha Press) by Dwight Okita. Copyright © 2002 by Dwight Okita. Used with permission of the author.

Plays Magazine for "Martin Luther King" by Aileen Fisher. Copyright © 1986. Reprinted by permission.

Random House, Inc., for "The Unknown Citizen" from *W. H. Auden: Collected Poems* by W. H. Auden. Copyright © 1976 by Edward Mendelson, William Meredith, and Monroe K. Spears, Executors of the Estate of W. H. Auden. Used by permission of Random House, Inc.

S©ott Treimel NY for "Enemies" by Charlotte Zolotow from *The Big Book for Peace*, edited by Ann Durell and Marilyn Sachs. Copyright © 1990 by Charlotte Zolotow. Reprinted by permission of S©ott Treimel NY.

Scribner for "America Was Schoolmasters" from *Collected Poems* by Robert P. Tristam Coffin. Copyright © 1943 by The Macmillan Company. Copyright renewed © 1971 by Margaret Coffin Halvosa, Mary Alice Westcott, Robert P. Tristam Coffin, Jr., and Richard N. Coffin. Reprinted with the permission of Scribner, an imprint of Simon & Schuster Adult Publishing Group.

Gregg Shapiro for "Tattoo" from *Troika II* by Carol L. Gloor, Janice Lynch, and Gregg Shapiro (Thorntree Press). Copyright © 1991 by Gregg Shapiro. By permission of the author.

The University of Arizona Press for "Occupant: Blue Roof Apartments" from *When Living Was a Labor Camp* by Diana García. Copyright © 2000 by Diana García. Reprinted by permission of the University of Arizona Press.

The University of Pittsburgh Press for "For Malcolm, a Year After" from *The Essential Etheridge Knight* by Etheridge Knight. Copyright © 1986. Reprinted by permission of the University of Pittsburgh Press.

Index of Titles and First Lines